Machine Learning with Clustering

A Visual Guide for Beginners with Examples in Python 3

Artem Kovera

CONTENTS

Introduction to machine learning and clustering

The amount of data in digital format has been growing exponentially in the last decades, and this tendency will certainly continue. Currently, data is a very valuable resource. For example, most companies collect various data, and some companies even sell data to other companies. Apparently, the success of any business in the near future will be largely determined by the efficiency of working with large amounts of data. But the data deluge is relevant not only to business; it is also extremely widespread in many other areas, such as science, education, medicine, state governance, and many others.

The discipline specifically designed to work with all sorts of data has been known for a long time. It is called statistics. However, traditional statistical approaches cannot be successfully applied to large amounts of data that we encounter today without using computational devices. And here comes to the rescue our hero – machine learning. Machine learning can be viewed as a form of applied statistics for solving various problems using computer algorithms. An algorithm is just a set of instructions.

However, even more importantly, machine learning gives computer programs another remarkable ability – the ability to adapt to changes in environment and learn from experience. This is the most important feature of machine learning.

In traditional programming approach, we explicitly give a computer a set of instructions to execute. In machine learning, we also give instructions (a machine learning algorithm) to a computer, but the algorithm generates a model on the data given to the computer, and then this model can make predictions on new data. That is how learning from previous experience comes into play.

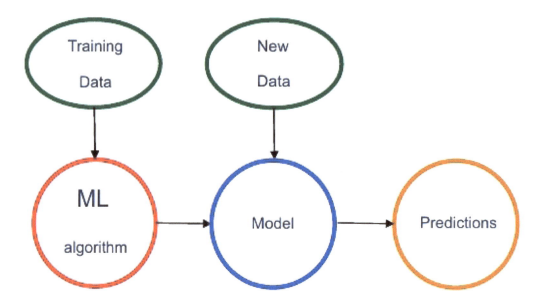

As you probably know, there are three major types of machine learning: supervised, unsupervised, and reinforcement machine learning.

In reinforcement learning, a machine learning agent or system has a goal or a set of goals. The agent observes its environment and has to decide what actions to take to achieve its goals. The agent gets a numerical reward whenever it chooses the actions that lead to achieving its goals.

Supervised learning is a type of learning, where pieces of the training data are labeled with descriptions or values. A very common type of supervised machine learning is classification. This approach has given plenty of practical achievements. But there is one problem with this kind of learning: we need humans to produce labeled data, and the production of such data becomes impractical and sometimes even virtually impossible for some types of data sets.

In the case of unsupervised learning, we do not have any labeled training data, and we need to extract some meaning from this unlabeled data.

Clustering algorithms belong to unsupervised machine learning. Cluster analysis or just clustering is basically a process of revealing hidden structures and patterns in datasets. Clustering can be viewed as an unlabeled search for similarity/dissimilarity among data points. The output of any cluster analysis is a model that divides the items in the data set into different clusters or classes. Because of this, clustering is also known as *unsupervised classification*.

Clustering algorithms have been applied in a plethora of various domains. Here, I will give you just a few examples.

In business, for instance, we can find different groups of customers sharing some similar features using cluster analysis. Then, we can use this information to develop different marketing strategies and apply them to all these separate groups of customers. Or, we can cluster a marketplace in a specific niche to find what kinds of products are selling better than other ones to make a decision what kind of products to produce.

The purpose of a very frequent application of clustering in various scientific disciplines is a construction of a hierarchy or taxonomy for some objects like biological organisms or types of galaxies in the cosmos. Also, for example, using clustering algorithms, scientists can identify similar groups of genes or discover some hidden structures in the universe like groups of galaxies, for example.

We could continue the list of different applications of clustering with hundreds of other examples. Speaking more generally and formally, there are four major tasks of clustering:

- *Making simplification for further data processing.* In this case, the data is split into different groups which then are processed individually. Our previous examples of clustering in business belong to this type. Usually, clustering is one of the first techniques that help explore a data set we are going to work with to get some sense of the structure of the data.
- *Compression of the data.* We can implement cluster analysis on a giant data set. Then from each cluster we can pick just several items. In this case, we usually lose much less information than in the case where we pick data points without preceding clustering. Clustering algorithms are being used to compress not only large data sets but also relatively small objects like images.
- *Picking out unusual data points from the dataset.* This procedure is done, for example, for the detection of fraud transactions with credit cards. In medicine,

similar procedures can be used, for example, to identify new forms of illnesses.

- **_Building a hierarchy of objects._** As we have just mentioned, this task is implemented for classification of biological organisms. It is also applied, for example, in search engines to group different text documents inside the search engines' datasets.

In any machine learning task, including clustering, we always work with some data. We can usually represent a data set in a tabular form. For example, here is a table of five data points from the dataset we will work with in the chapter on the k-means algorithm:

Country	Control of Corruption	Government Effectiveness	Political Stability	Regulatory Quality	Rule of Law	Voice and Accountabil
Afghanistan	-1.340411	-1.335604	-2.502350	-1.008351	-1.592565	-1.152
Albania	-0.444014	0.027830	0.357206	0.198663	-0.359367	0.159
Algeria	-0.681529	-0.506218	-1.046453	-1.169924	-0.831184	-0.852
Andorra	1.246003	1.752355	1.436771	0.892059	1.594601	1.208
Angola	-1.396893	-1.012036	-0.590507	-0.908264	-1.069294	-1.185

In this table, each country represents a _data point_, and each column ('Control of Corruption', 'Government Effectiveness', etc) represents an entity with several different names: _feature, variable, dimension,_ or _attribute_. We can see that we have six features in this data set.

There are different types of features, but in this book we will work only with numeric features.

As we said, clustering is all about finding similarity among data points and collecting them in groups or clusters based on this similarity. In order to measure similarity between data points, we use special characteristics called metrics or distance functions. There are quite a few of possible metrics.

The most frequently used metrics in clustering algorithms are the following:

- *Euclidean distance;*
- *Murkowski distance;*
- *Manhattan distance.*

There is no best type of a metric in general, but the Euclidean distance is the simplest, most common, and, probably, most intuitive type. Basically, it's just a length of a straight line between two points. We will use the Euclidean distance in all algorithms in this book.

One important aspect of using the Euclidian distance is that we often need to normalize our data. Which means different features must be in the same range of values. Otherwise, the features with bigger ranges of values would be more significant than other features.

The Euclidean distance *d* between the points **M** $(m_1, m_2, \ldots m_n)$ and **K** $(k_1, k_2, \ldots k_n)$ is given by the formula:

$$d = \sqrt{(k_1 - m_1)^2 + (k_2 - m_2)^2 + \ldots + (k_n - m_n)^2}$$

, where *n* is the number of dimensions of the space.

For example, in a 2-dimentional space, the Euclidian distance *d* between the points **A** (1, 1) and **B** (7, 9) in the picture below is equal to

$$d = \sqrt{(7 - 1)^2 + (9 - 1)^2} = 10$$

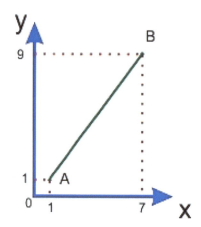

Let's imagine that we wanted to calculate the Euclidian distance **d** in a 5-dimensional space between the points **C** (1, 12, 5, 6, 41) and **F** (3, 10, 11, 0, 49). In this case, we would have:

$$d = \sqrt{(3-1)^2 + (10-12)^2 + (11-5)^2 + (0-6)^2 + (49-41)^2} = 12$$

If you are an absolute beginner in data science or just simply not well-versed in math, I should probably say a few words about the notion of dimensionality. If we have a dataset whose data points have 2 features, we are working with 2-dimensional space, which is a plane. Not surprisingly, we can easily visualize a plane. Also, we can visualize a 3-dimentsonal space. But we cannot imagine or appropriately visualize more than 3-dimensional spaces. However, in data science, we often need to work with such higher dimensional spaces. Although we cannot visualize more than 3-dimensional spaces, we can easily work with them algebraically as we've just done for calculating the Euclidian distance in a 5-dimensional space. I hope it is absolutely clear to you.

Also, we should introduce a rather frightening term *"the curse of dimensionality"*, which is a very common term in machine learning jargon. The occurrence of the curse of dimensionality has a couple of different prerequisites. First, adding extra dimensions to the data set increases the probability of adding noise, and this noise can then obscure and even completely change the results. However, in some cases, adding *relevant* features will make the separation of the clusters easier. Second, and probably even more importantly, as the number of features of dimensions grows, the data points in the data set are becoming more widely spread out. In this situation, the number of the data points has to grow exponentially if we want to produce accurate models. And, at some point, this growth of the dataset becomes impractical. Besides, working with higher dimensional data always requires using more computational resources. That is why data scientists do not usually like to work with data, say, with dozens let alone hundreds of dimensions. The curse of dimensionality is not only relevant to clustering, but also to all other types of machine learning tasks.

If we maximize the dissimilarity among clusters in our data, we will get the scenario, where each cluster consists of a single data point:

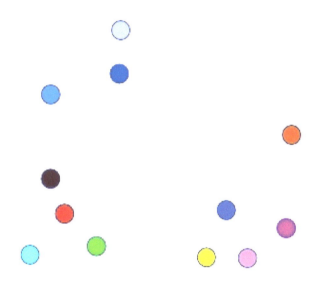

In machine learning, such a situation is known as *overfitting*. Overfitting refers to a model that is too specific and cannot be applied to new data. In clustering, we can get around this problem by applying some constraints in the parameters of the algorithms. It can be some value of a minimum distance between clusters or some specified number of clusters.

Conversely, when our model is too general, all the data tend to be assigned to a single cluster. This is known as *underfitting*:

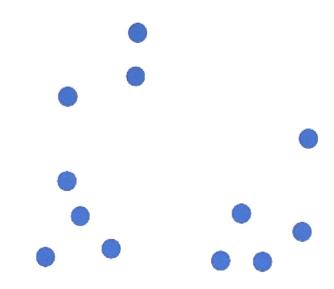

Obviously, an underfitting model is not suitable either. If underfitting takes place, we can also get around this by changing some parameters in our algorithm.

There is always some level of subjectivity in all clustering tasks. There are many different ways of clustering the same data.

For example, we have a collection of data points on the picture below:

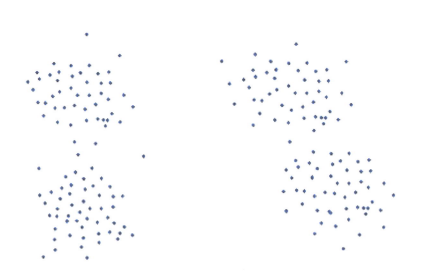

We could divide these data points into two clusters:

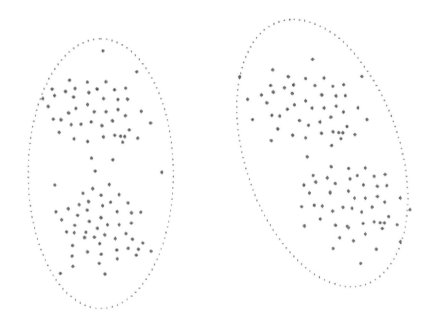

But we could also divide them into four clusters:

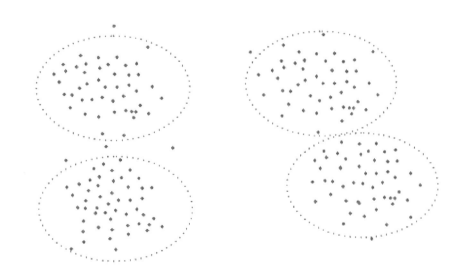

There are hundreds of different clustering algorithms, which can fall into many different categories in several different ways. One way to categorize clustering algorithms is by what kind of overlapping they impose over the data:

- *Hard clustering.* In this approach, clusters cannot overlap: each data point belongs to only one cluster. In this book, we will mainly discuss the most commonly used hard clustering algorithms.
- *Soft clustering.* In this type of clustering, clusters can overlap: a single data point can belong to multiple clusters.

Having discussed some basics ideas of machine learning and cluster analysis, we are now ready to delve into specific clustering algorithms.

Hierarchical clustering

The main idea and advantages/disadvantages of the algorithm

We'll begin our tour with hierarchical clustering. This type of clustering is all about finding hierarchy in data sets. Based on this hierarchy, different items in the data set can be allocated to separate clusters.

Unlike the k-means method, which we will cover in the next chapter, the hierarchical clustering is a deterministic type of clustering: no matter where we are starting, we are always obtaining the same results.

The outcome of hierarchical clustering can be represented by a tree-like structure called a dendrogram. The root of this structure is the cluster that gathers all the samples. The height in the dendrogram represents the distance between clusters in the data space.

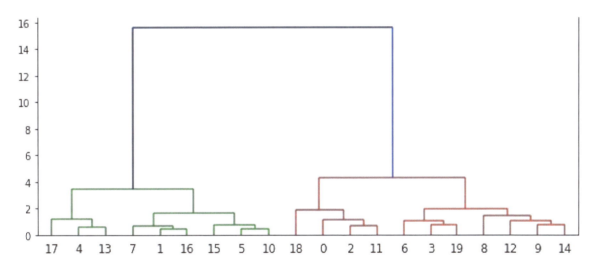

We have two possible strategies: *agglomerative clustering* (bottom-up) and *divisive clustering* (top-down). Agglomerative clustering is a far more common hierarchical approach because divisive clustering is a prohibitively computationally expensive procedure, usually with time complexity $2^{n-1}-1$, where n is the number of the data points.

In agglomerative clustering, each sample is initially a cluster. Then, at each step we find two closest samples and combine them in a new, larger cluster until we have only one agglomerative cluster at the top.

In divisive hierarchical clustering (the top-down approach), we use another approach that works in an opposite direction: in this method we start with the all-inclusive cluster (the whole data set) and successively split it until all the data points represent individual clusters.

In both hierarchical clustering methods, we obtain a dendrogram with one cluster at the top, and we can cut the dendrogram in different places to get different numbers of clusters. But, how do we choose the optimal number of clusters in the dendrogram to divide the data set? In some cases, such as taxonomy, our task is to represent the complete or almost complete structure of the dendrogram, so we do not split the dendrogram at all. In some other cases, we know the number of clusters in advance to split the dendrogram. In many other cases, the best choice of the ultimate number of clusters is the minimum number of the vertical lines in the dendrogram cut by a horizontal line that intersects the vertical line corresponding to the maximum distance.

For example, according to this method, the optimal number of clusters in this dendrogram equals two:

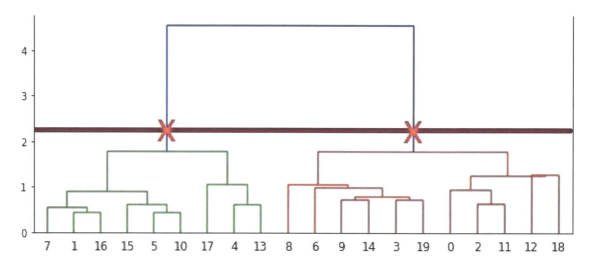

Some other heuristic methods can also be applied to determine the optimal number of clusters.

Hierarchical clustering algorithms can be used in many domains, but the most common use of these algorithms is in science.

Although agglomerative clustering is more computationally efficient than the divisive method, agglomerative clustering algorithms are still quite complex computational procedures, which can be impractical on very large datasets.

Different metrics for computing the distance between clusters

What do we mean by the *distance* between clusters? There are multiple definitions of distance. They are called linkage metrics. In the introductory chapter, we introduced some metrics to measure the distance between data points. Here, instead, we will introduce some commonly used metrics to measure the distance between clusters:

❖ **single linkage** or MIN metric is a distance between two closest points in two different clusters:

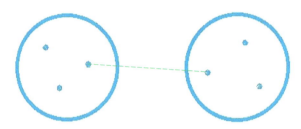

❖ **complete linkage** or MAX metric is a distance between the farthest two points:

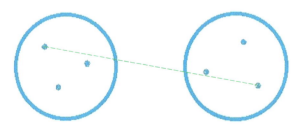

❖ **average distance** is a distance calculated as average of all pairs of points from two different clusters:

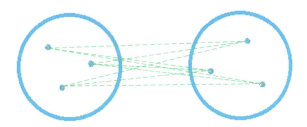

❖ **centroid distance** is a distance between the centers of two clusters:

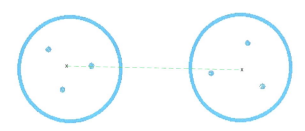

❖ **Ward's distance** is calculated as a centroid distance multiplied by a special parameter.

There is no ideal linkage metric, but, in most cases, Ward's distance is a more preferable metric than the other ones.

Hierarchical agglomerative clustering with the SciPy library

So, let's write a simple program in Python which will execute hierarchical agglomerative clustering.

Python is a great programming language. Programs in Python are usually easy to write and read. However, using pure Python is not a very effective strategy for most mathematic operations. That is why, dealing with mathematical tasks, such as machine learning, python programmers use some very useful libraries, such as Numpy, Scipy, Scikit-learn, and some others. Using such libraries makes programmers' work much easier because it is much less code to write and read. Especially, it is very important for beginners, who can easily get lost in long sheets of code. Also, which is even more importantly for large-scale practical tasks, using such libraries usually makes programs sufficiently faster. In this book, we will be using these libraries almost everywhere.

Probably, the easiest way to write an agglomerative clustering program in Python is to use a very common python library for scientific computing, called SciPy.

First of all, let's import all packages we need:

```
import pandas as pd
import matplotlib.pyplot as plt
from scipy.cluster.hierarchy import dendrogram, linkage
```

Then, we should import our dataset. I prepared a dataset from World Bank's open data http://data.worldbank.org/. I got the dataset called Worldwide Governance Indicators for 2015 year and prepared a smaller dataset of 20 countries because smaller dendrograms would be represented in this book better. You can also play around with a dataset of 195 countries available at:

https://raw.githubusercontent.com/ArtemKovera/clust/master/datacountries.csv

So, let's import the data:

```
X=pd.read_table("https://raw.githubusercontent.com/ArtemKovera/clust/master/datacountriesshort.csv", sep=";")
X
```

Then a nice table shows up. This is our data we will work with:

	Country	Control of Corruption	Government Effectiveness	Political Stability	Regulatory Quality	Rule of Law	Voice and Accountability
0	Armenia	-0.451385	-0.135415	-0.291859	0.248901	-0.343095	-0.536519
1	Belgium	1.582632	1.441359	0.603097	1.277324	1.421055	1.392743
2	Brazil	-0.432713	-0.189014	-0.379241	-0.212530	-0.192782	0.383081
3	Chad	-1.292505	-1.450364	-0.986351	-1.196029	-1.161228	-1.351856
4	Czech Republic	0.390839	1.051496	0.959901	1.084800	1.123225	1.019538
5	Finland	2.283533	1.822501	1.038719	1.828457	2.073493	1.560110
6	Haiti	-1.257345	-2.002146	-0.729088	-1.159087	-1.166457	-0.836118
7	Japan	1.608630	1.791388	0.977663	1.177005	1.511390	1.022507
8	Liberia	-0.610637	-1.367291	-0.738625	-0.881921	-0.870829	-0.258795
9	Mauritania	-0.906050	-1.028588	-0.656419	-0.858530	-0.820225	-0.907473
10	Netherlands	1.892111	1.841793	0.929998	1.768844	1.934686	1.569623
11	Philippines	-0.430052	0.107092	-0.838326	-0.036930	-0.345095	0.136829
12	Russian Federation	-0.862619	-0.182620	-1.049051	-0.522403	-0.719673	-1.067474
13	Slovenia	0.726810	0.973970	0.919430	0.620738	0.953715	0.945217
14	Tajikistan	-0.997935	-0.819396	-0.866736	-1.006108	-1.009642	-1.512956
15	United Kingdom	1.867393	1.738755	0.556856	1.855618	1.805057	1.270090
16	United States	1.378527	1.461995	0.699095	1.297577	1.603706	1.075170
17	Uruguay	1.298154	0.540124	0.989900	0.452428	0.675225	1.121650
18	Vietnam	-0.447043	0.076964	0.010676	-0.496354	-0.268542	-1.328915
19	Zimbabwe	-1.286892	-1.147969	-0.577252	-1.646901	-1.349086	-1.192694

We do not need to normalize these data points now because all the features were at the same range in the original dataset.

Then, we should cut out the column with a string variable:

```
df.drop('Country', axis=1, inplace=True)
```

Then, we put our data in the variable X:

```
X=df
```

Now, we are ready to implement the clustering algorithm:

```
Z = linkage(X, 'complete')
plt.figure(figsize=(10, 4))
dendrogram(Z)
plt.title('Hierarchical Clustering Dendrogram - Complete Linkage')
plt.show()
```

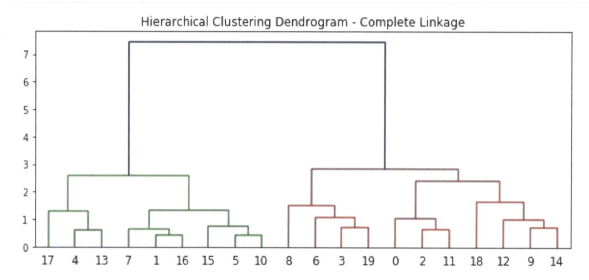

A few lines of code, and we see our first results. The numbers below the dendrogram indicate different countries in our dataset.

Now let's use several other linkage metrics:

```
Z = linkage(X, 'single')
plt.figure(figsize=(10, 4))
dendrogram(Z)
plt.title('Hierarchical Clustering Dendrogram - Single Linkage')
plt.show()
```

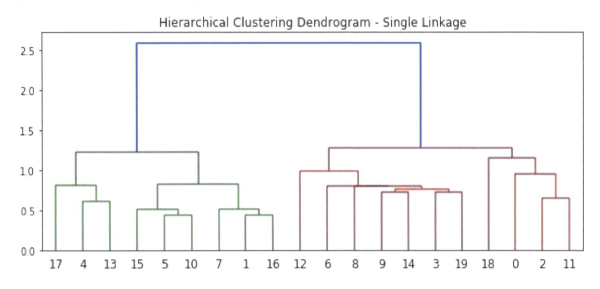

```
Z = linkage(X, 'average')
plt.figure(figsize=(10, 4))
dendrogram(Z)
plt.title('Hierarchical Clustering Dendrogram - Average Linkage')
plt.show()
```

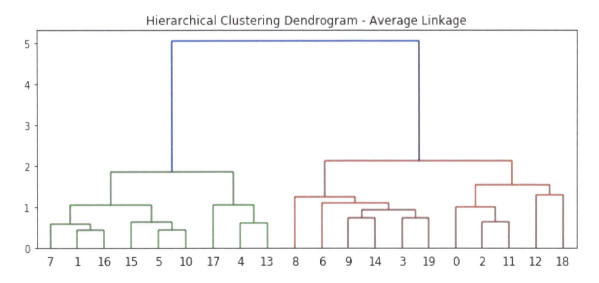

```
Z = linkage(X, 'ward')
plt.figure(figsize=(10, 4))
dendrogram(Z)
plt.title('Hierarchical Clustering Dendrogram - Ward Linkage')
plt.show()
```

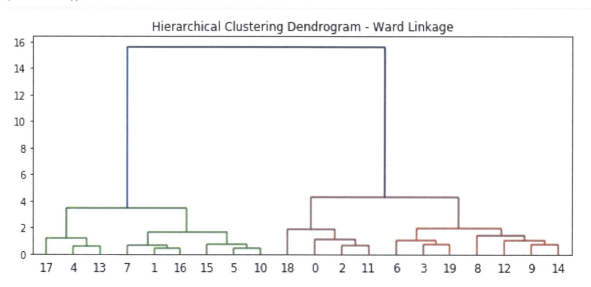

As we see, the results are very similar. All four dendrograms produce two major clusters, and, in all four cases, these two major clusters consist of the same countries. However, the structures of the major clusters differ depending on a linkage metric.

K-means algorithm

The main principles of the algorithm

The K-means algorithm is one of the oldest and most commonly used clustering algorithms. This algorithm belongs to so-called partitional clustering methods. In the name of this algorithm, *k* refers to the number of clusters.

In contrast to hierarchical clustering, in the K-means algorithm, we specify the number of clusters beforehand.

The logic of the algorithm can be described in the following steps:

1) Place k centroids at random locations. (There is a version of k-means, where the centroids are initialized not completely randomly, called k-means++) The number of clusters we will have at the end equals the number of the centroids:

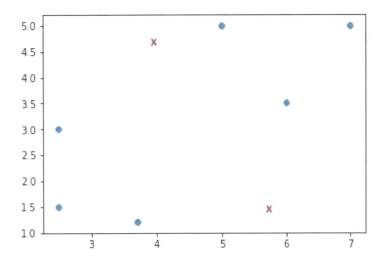

2) For each data point, find the nearest centroid:

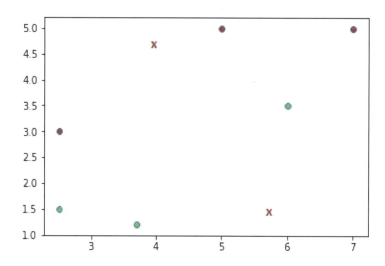

3) Recompute the positions of the centroids. (Find the average centers of the gravity, in this example for the green and red points):

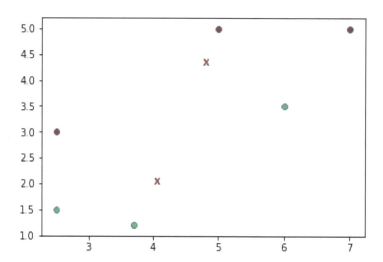

4) Reassign the data points to the nearest centroids:

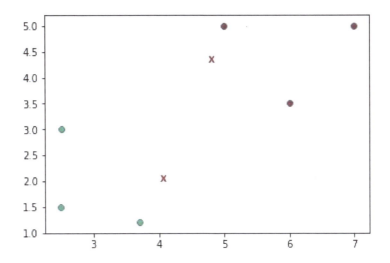

5) Again recompute the positions of the centroids:

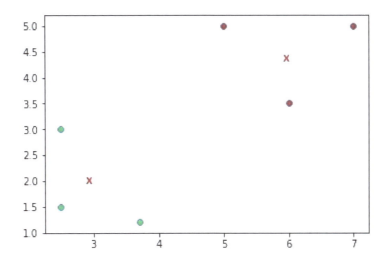

6) Repeat the steps 4 and 5 until no improvements are possible and the centroids do not move.

The k-means algorithm is much faster than the majority of other clustering algorithms. The time complexity of this algorithm is generally $O(n)$. However, we need to specify and limit to some value the number of conversions in the algorithm because this number can be unreasonably large: as the algorithm progresses, in some cases, (especially on very large datasets) the centroids may start moving to their final locations at infinitesimally small steps, and we can simply ignore those final iterations without damaging our results greatly.

Implementing k-means using the Scikit-learn library

In the example of hierarchical clustering, we worked with a data set of 20 countries. This time, we will be working with a data set of 195 countries. We will be using the K-means algorithm from the Scikit-learn library.

As always, first we import all packages and data we need:

```
import pandas as pd
from sklearn.cluster import KMeans
import matplotlib.pyplot as plt

X=pd.read_table("https://raw.githubusercontent.com/ArtemKovera/clust/master/db2.csv", sep=";")
```

Set the values of the 'Country' column as indexes:

```
X.set_index('Country', inplace=True)
```

Then, we implement the algorithm. We create our k-means object and feed our data into this object:

```
km=KMeans(n_clusters=2) #n_clusters - the number of clusters
km.fit(X)
```

Finally, show the results:

```
Results = dict(zip(X.index,km.labels_))
print (Results)
```

{'Afghanistan': 1, 'Albania': 1, 'Algeria': 1, 'Andorra': 0, 'Angola': 1, 'Antigua and Barbuda': 0, 'Argentina': 1, 'Armenia': 1, 'Aruba': 0, 'Australia': 0, 'Austria': 0, 'Azerbaijan': 1, 'Bahamas. The': 0, 'Bahrain': 1, 'Bangladesh': 1, 'Barbados': 0, 'Belarus': 1, 'Belgium': 0, 'Belize': 1, 'Benin': 1, 'Bhutan': 0, 'Bolivia': 1, 'Bosnia and Herzegovina': 1, 'Botswana': 0, 'Brazil': 1, 'Brunei Darussalam': 0, 'Bulgaria': 1, 'Burkina Faso': 1, 'Burundi': 1, 'Cabo Verde': 0, 'Cambodia': 1, 'Cameroon': 1, 'Canada': 0, 'Cayman Islands': 0, 'Central African Republic': 1, 'Chad': 1, 'Chile': 0, 'China': 1, 'Colombia': 1, 'Comoros': 1, 'Congo. Dem. Rep.': 1, 'Congo. Rep.': 1, 'Costa Rica': 0, "Cote d'Ivoire": 1, 'Croatia': 0, 'Cuba': 1, 'Cyprus': 0, 'Czech Republic': 0, 'Denmark': 0, 'Djibouti': 1, 'Dominica': 0, 'Dominican Republic': 1, 'Ecuador': 1, 'Egypt. Arab Rep.': 1, 'El Salvador': 1, 'Equatorial Guinea': 1, 'Eritrea': 1, 'Estonia': 0, 'Ethiopia': 1, 'Fiji': 1, 'Finland': 0, 'France': 0, 'French Guiana': 0, 'Gabon': 1, 'Gambia. The': 1, 'Georgia': 0, 'Germany': 0, 'Ghana': 1, 'Greece': 1, 'Greenland': 0, 'Grenada': 0, 'Guatemala': 1, 'Guinea': 1, 'Guinea-Bissau': 1, 'Guyana': 1, 'Haiti': 1, 'Honduras': 1, 'Hong Kong SAR. China': 0, 'Hungary': 0, 'Iceland': 0, 'India': 1, 'Indonesia': 1, 'Iran. Islamic Rep.': 1, 'Iraq': 1, 'Ireland': 0, 'Israel': 0, 'Italy': 0, 'Jamaica': 1, 'Japan': 0, 'Jersey. Channel Islands': 0, 'Jordan': 1, 'Kazakhstan': 1, 'Kenya': 1, 'Kiribati': 1, 'Korea. Dem. People?s Rep.': 1, 'Korea. Rep.': 0, 'Kosovo': 1, 'Kuwait': 1, 'Kyrgyz Republic': 1, 'Lao PDR': 1, 'Latvia': 0, 'Lebanon': 1, 'Lesotho': 1, 'Liberia': 1, 'Libya': 1, 'Liechtenstein': 0, 'Lithuania': 0, 'Luxembourg': 0, 'Macao SAR. China': 0, 'Macedonia. FYR': 1, 'Madagascar': 1, 'Malawi': 1, 'Malaysia': 0, 'Maldives': 1, 'Mali': 1, 'Malta': 0, 'Marshall Islands': 1, 'Mauritania': 1, 'Mauritius': 0, 'Mexico': 1, 'Micronesia. Fed. Sts.': 1, 'Moldova': 1, 'Mongolia': 1, 'Montenegro': 1, 'Morocco': 1, 'Mozambique': 1, 'Myanmar': 1, 'Namibia': 0, 'Nauru': 1, 'Nepal': 1, 'Netherlands': 0, 'New Zealand': 0, 'Nicaragua': 1, 'Niger': 1, 'Nigeria': 1, 'Norway': 0, 'Oman': 1, 'Pakistan': 1, 'Palau': 1, 'Panama': 1, 'Papua New Guinea': 1, 'Paraguay': 1, 'Peru': 1, 'Philippines': 1, 'Poland': 0, 'Portugal': 0, 'Puerto Rico': 0, 'Qatar': 0, 'Romania': 1, 'Russian Federation': 1, 'Rwanda': 1, 'Samoa': 1, 'Saudi Arabia': 1, 'Senegal': 1, 'Serbia': 1, 'Seychelles': 0, 'Sierra Leone': 1, 'Singapore': 0, 'Slovak Republic': 0, 'Slovenia': 0, 'Somalia': 1, 'South Africa': 1, 'South Sudan': 1, 'Spain': 0, 'Sri Lanka': 1, 'Sudan': 1, 'Suriname': 1, 'Swaziland': 1, 'Sweden': 0, 'Switzerland': 0, 'Syrian Arab Republic': 1, 'Taiwan. China': 0, 'Tajikistan': 1, 'Tanzania': 1, 'Thailand': 1, 'Timor-Leste': 1, 'Togo': 1, 'Tonga': 1, 'Trinidad and Tobago': 1, 'Tunisia': 1, 'Turkey': 1, 'Turkmenistan': 1, 'Tuvalu': 1, 'Uganda': 1, 'Ukraine': 1, 'United Arab Emirates': 0, 'United Kingdom': 0, 'United States': 0, 'Uruguay': 0, 'Uzbekistan': 1, 'Vanuatu': 1, 'Venezuela. RB': 1, 'Vietnam': 1, 'Yemen. Rep.': 1, 'Zambia': 1, 'Zimbabwe': 1}

Besides **n_clusters**, the K-means algorithm in the Scikit-learn library has a bunch of other parameters we can tune, which you can check out in the documentation: http://scikit-learn.org/stable/modules/generated/sklearn.cluster.KMeans.html .

Here we will discuss a few of them.

As we have seen, the number of iteration of the k-means algorithm can be unreasonably large. The parameter **max_iter** deals with this problem. This parameter is the maximum number of iterations of the algorithm for a single run. The default value of this parameter is 300.

The parameter **init** specifies the method for choosing initial positions of the centroids. The default value of this parameter is "k-means++". This method initiates the centroids in a smart way to speed up convergence and increase the probability of obtaining more meaningful results.

The main idea behind k-means++ initialization is that the centroids are getting spread out more widely than in most instances of random k-means initialization. In the k-means++ approach, the first centroid is initialized randomly from among the data points. Then, for each data point x, the algorithm computes the distance $D(x)$ between x and the nearest centroid that has already been chosen. The highest probability of choosing the next centroid corresponds to the farthest data point from the first centroid: the more the distance $D(x)$, the higher the probability for a data point to become the next centroid. Then, the algorithm recomputes the $D(x)$ for each x from two previous centroids. Again, the highest probability of choosing the third centroid corresponds to the farthest data point from the first and second centroids. The algorithm iterates the steps of recomputing the distance $D(x)$ and choosing centroids until all the k centroids are initialized.

Another value for the **init** parameter is "random", in which all the centroids are initialized at random locations. Also, this parameter allows us to initialize the centroids manually.

The parameter **n_init** determines how many times the k-means algorithm will be run with different centroid seeds. The default value of this parameter equals 10. In principle, the higher this parameter is set, the longer the implementation of the algorithm, but it is likelier that the algorithm will give more appropriate results.

The disadvantages of k-means and methods to overcome them

Although the k-means algorithm has some important advantages over other clustering methods, this algorithm has also a number of drawbacks.

The first disadvantage of this algorithm is that depending on the initial positions of the centroids, we can have dramatically different results at the end. So, the k-means algorithm is not deterministic. Also, there is no guarantee that the algorithm will converge to the global optimum. We can partially get around these problems by running the algorithm multiple times and picking the output with the smallest variance. Another solution to this problem is using k-means++ initialization. It is better to use both these methods simultaneously, like we just did using Scikit-learn k-means.

The second and probably most important disadvantage of the k-means algorithm is that we have to specify the number of clusters in advance.

Having some *a priori* knowledge about the problem can help choose *k* – the number of clusters. Sometimes we indeed have such knowledge. For example, in clustering astrophysical images, it is known beforehand that there are two types of brightest objects in the cosmos: galaxies and quasars, so we can determine the number of clusters as two.

When we don't have enough prior knowledge about the problem, we need to search for a good *k*. We can implement the algorithm for different values of *k* and compare the variances of the clusters we get. But in this case, it turns out that the more the clusters, the lower the variance, and, because of this, the best number of clusters is the number of the data points, but it doesn't make sense, of course.

Instead of choosing the results with the lowest variance, we can use the *Elbow method*. In this method, we run the K-means algorithm with different values of *k*. We should use the number of clusters such that adding another cluster does not give a substantial difference between the sum of squared errors or, in other words, the ratio of the between-group variance to the total variance.

In the example of using the *Elbow method,* we will be using the K-means algorithm from the Scikit-learn library and the function **cdist** for distance computation from the Scipy library:

```python
from sklearn.cluster import KMeans
from scipy.spatial.distance import cdist
import numpy as np
import matplotlib.pyplot as plt
```

Then, we initialize our data set and plot it:

```python
x1=np.array([1.4, 2, 1.5, 1.9, 2.1, 1.9, 2.2, 2.7, 2.2, 2.5, 2.4, 1.7, 2.3, 2.1, 1.6,
             4.9, 4.7, 4, 4.1, 4.2, 4.6, 4.7, 5.1, 5.3, 5.4, 4.1, 4.5, 4.6, 4.5, 3.8,
             3.5, 4, 4.5, 3.7, 3.7, 3.6, 3.5, 3.6, 3.7, 3.7, 3.8, 3.9, 4, 4.2, 3.9, 3.7])
x2=np.array([2, 1.4, 1.5, 6, 3, 4, 5, 7, 7.2, 7.5, 6, 2, 4, 2.3, 2.8,
             8, 7, 1, 2, 3, 4, 5, 6, 7, 8, 5.3, 4.5, 5.8, 2.8, 2.4,
             10, 13, 13.2, 11, 8.8, 8.4, 8.9, 10.2, 11.1, 11.7, 12.4, 12.8, 11, 12.5, 11.6, 10.1])

plt.scatter(x1, x2)
plt.show()
```

As a result, we get this plot:

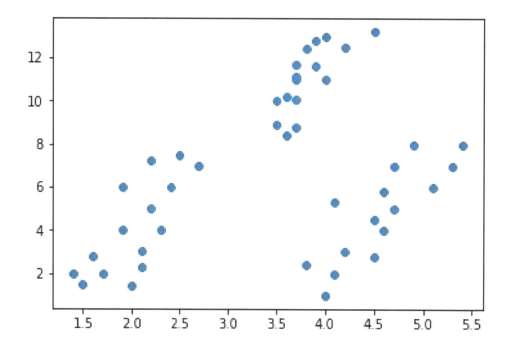

Then, we write the following code:

```
X = np.array(list(zip(x1, x2)))


Distance = []
for k in range(1,10):
    km = KMeans(n_clusters=k).fit(X)
    km.fit(X)
    Distance.append(sum(np.min(cdist(X, km.cluster_centers_, 'euclidean'), axis=1)) / X.shape[1])

plt.plot(K, Distance, 'bx-')
plt.xlabel('Number of clusters')
plt.ylabel('Distance')
```

Finally, we can see the results of the elbow method:

```
plt.show()
```

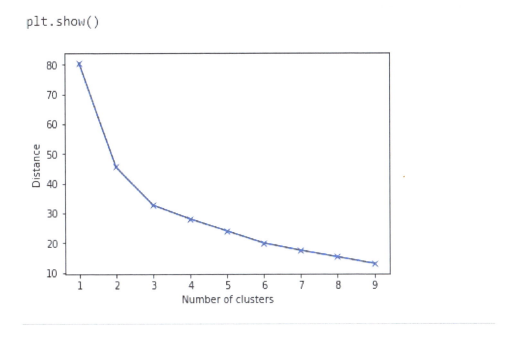

In this example, according to the elbow method, it seems that the best number of clusters is three.

In addition to such technique as the elbow method, we can determine the appropriate number of clusters just by exploring the visual representation of our data. Personally, I prefer visualization to the elbow method.

If we are working with high-dimensional data, we need to use the process known as *dimensionality reduction* in order to be able to visualize the data. The discussion of dimensionality reduction methods lies beyond the scope of this book. Here I will just say that one common strategy to reduce the dimensionality of the data is to combine several features which correlate with each other. The principal component analysis (PCA) and the distributed stochastic neighbor embedding (T-SNE) are commonly used algorithms for implementing dimensionality reduction. Self-organizing maps, which we'll cover later, are also an effective tool for dimensionality reduction and data visualization.

Also, for determining the right number of clusters, we can take a random sample of our data and use hierarchical clustering on it.

The k-means algorithm is susceptible to noise in the dataset: in some cases, even a few outliers can distort the results greatly. We can overcome this problem by eliminating the data points whose contribution in the sum of the squared error (SSE) is very large, especially over multiple runs.

The next disadvantage of the k-means algorithm is that this algorithm can give appropriate results only when the clusters tend to have spherical shapes. In other cases, the algorithm can produce counterintuitive results like in the picture below:

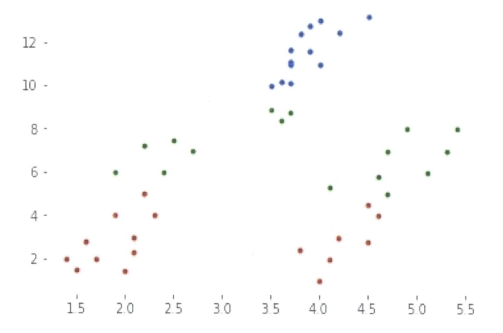

Obviously, this outcome is not what we would like to have. In such situations, we should use different methods, such as the DBSCAN clustering algorithm.

Introduction to the expectation–maximization (EM) algorithm

At the end of this chapter, we should say that there is a soft clustering algorithm which is very similar to the k-means algorithm. This algorithm is called an expectation–maximization (EM) algorithm. The EM algorithm assumes that the data represent a mixture of different Gaussian distributions. This means that all the data points have certain probabilities of belonging to these Gaussian distributions.

The Gaussian distribution, also known as the normal distribution is a very common type of continuous distributions. It is called normal because when the number of observations is sufficiently large, the values of the outcomes become normally distributed. Many processes in the real physical world can be viewed as nearly normal distributions.

If we have one-dimensional feature space, the normal distribution can be represented as a bell curve. The curve is taller in the middle.

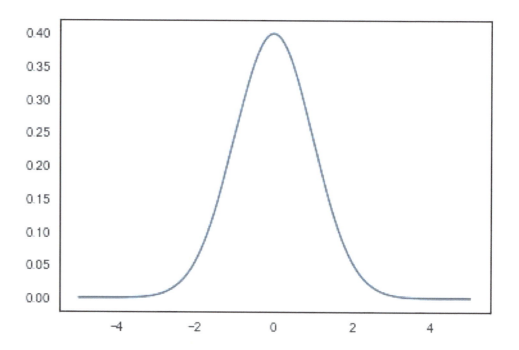

We need only two parameters to define Gaussian distribution: mean and standard deviation. The normal distribution is average about its mean. The standard deviation determines a shape of Gaussian distribution curve. If the standard deviation is smaller, the bell of the curve is narrower and taller.

Under the curve there is a probability area. The cumulative probabilities of different intervals of values correspond to the areas under the curve. Both to the right and to the left from the mean, the cumulative probabilities are equal to 0.5. Given the mean and standard deviation, we can find a cumulative probability of any interval of the normal distribution curve.

Sometimes several different Gaussian distributions can be found in the data set. Such representation of data is called a Gaussian mixture model. Any Gaussian mixture model consists of a finite number of separate Gaussian distributions.

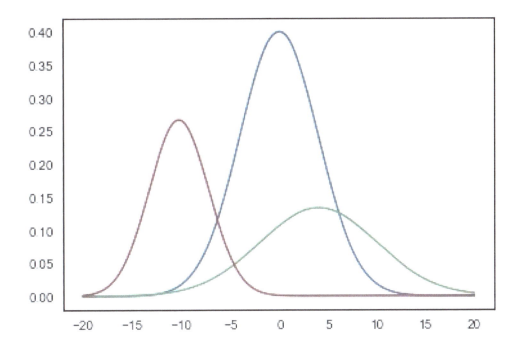

The expectation-maximization (EM) algorithm is used to find the probabilities for the data points to belong to given Gaussian distributions in a Gaussian mixture model.

The EM algorithm is an iterative process, which starts off with a random or heuristic initialization (just like in k-means). After the initialization of the centroids, the algorithm iteratively performs two steps: E-step and M-step.

For each data point, the E-step computes the probabilities of belonging to each of the clusters.

The M-step updates the parameters of the clusters (mean and covariance) based on the data assignments made in a previous E-step.

The algorithm stops when the parameters of the clusters no longer change.

Like in the k-means algorithm, we have to specify in advance how many distributions or clusters we have.

DBSCAN

The main principles of the algorithm

Hierarchical clustering and partitial clustering approaches such as k-means are based on finding similarities between data points. However, there are other alternatives to similarity-based clustering. One of them is density-based clustering. The density-based spatial clustering of applications with noise (DBSCAN) algorithm belongs to the group of density-based clustering algorithms.

DBSCAN is a relatively new and popular clustering algorithm, which has some important advantages over many other clustering algorithms.

In density-based clustering, a cluster is defined as a composition of density-connected points. There are several different methods for defining *density* in density-based clustering algorithms. DBSCAN uses the center-based approach. As output, the DBSCAN algorithm returns a set of clusters which are dense areas separated by less dense areas.

DBSCAN has two main parameters that we specify: *epsilon* and *minpts*.

The epsilon in DBSCAN is basically a certain value of the distance around each data point.

The minpts is a minimum number of points within the epsilon.

In the DBSCAN algorithm, all data points are divided into three categories: core, border, and noise points.

A core point is any point which has at least minpts points in its epsilon.

A border point is a non-core point which has at least one core point in its epsilon.

A noise point is neither a core nor border point.

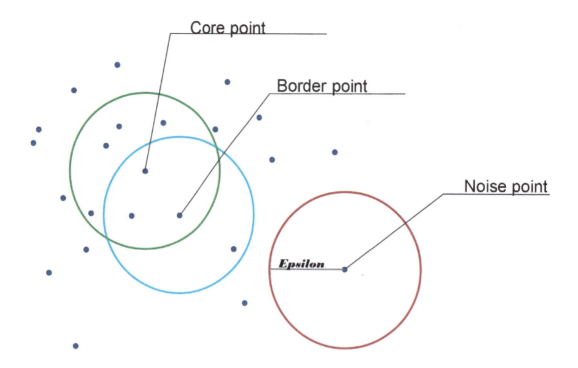

The DBSCAN algorithm can be described as follows.

1. Define all the points as core, border, or noise point.
2. Eliminate all the noise points.
3. Make each group of the core points that lie within *epsilons* of one another into a separate cluster.
4. Assign each border point to one of the clusters of its associated core points.

Implementing DBSCAN using the Scikit-learn library

As always, we import all the packages we need and initialize our data set. It is equivalent to the data set from one previous k-means example:

```
from sklearn.cluster import DBSCAN
import numpy as np
import matplotlib.pyplot as plt
```

```
x1=np.array([1.4, 2, 1.5, 1.9, 2.1, 1.9, 2.2, 2.7, 2.2, 2.5, 2.4, 1.7, 2.3, 2.1, 1.6,
             4.9, 4.7, 4, 4.1, 4.2, 4.6, 4.7, 5.1, 5.3, 5.4, 4.1, 4.5, 4.6, 4.5, 3.8,
             3.5, 4, 4.5, 3.7, 3.7, 3.6, 3.5, 3.6, 3.7, 3.7, 3.8, 3.9, 4, 4.2, 3.9, 3.7])
x2=np.array([2, 1.4, 1.5, 6, 3, 4, 5, 7, 7.2, 7.5, 6, 2, 4, 2.3, 2.8,
             8, 7, 1, 2, 3, 4, 5, 6, 7, 8, 5.3, 4.5, 5.8, 2.8, 2.4,
             10, 13, 13.2, 11, 8.8, 8.4, 8.9, 10.2, 11.1, 11.7, 12.4, 12.8, 11, 12.5, 11.6, 10.1])
```

```
plt.scatter(x1, x2)
plt.show()
```

Put our data in the variable X and implement the DBSCAN algorithm:

```
X = np.array(list(zip(x1, x2)))
dbscan = DBSCAN(eps=1.3, min_samples=3).fit(X)
```

Then, we call the attribute "**labels_**" and see that we have three clusters (0, 1, 2):

```
dbscan.labels_
array([0, 0, 0, 0, 0, 0, 0, 0, 0, 0, 0, 0, 0, 0, 0, 1, 1, 1, 1, 1, 1, 1, 1,
       1, 1, 1, 1, 1, 1, 1, 2, 2, 2, 2, 2, 2, 2, 2, 2, 2, 2, 2, 2, 2, 2, 2], dtype=int64)
```

Finally, we plot our results:

```
colors = ["g.", "r.", "b."]
for i in range(len(X)) :

    plt.plot(X[i][0], X[i][1], colors[dbscan.labels_[i]])
```

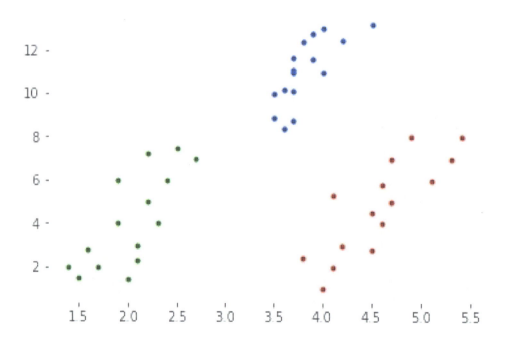

The output of DBSCAN is certainly more preferable than the one obtained for the same data by the k-means algorithm:

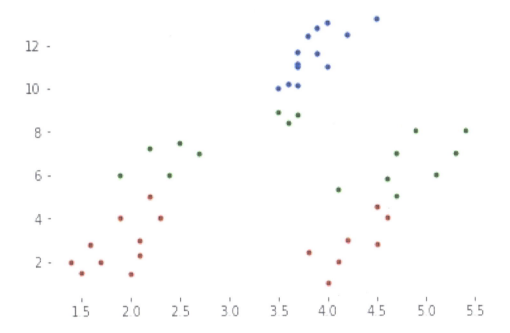

Advantages and disadvantages of DBSCAN

As we said, DBSCAN has several very important advantages over many other clustering algorithms.

First, we don't have to specify in advance how many clusters we are looking for. Second, DBSCAN can eliminate noise points, which are very common in real-world data sets. Also, this algorithm can detect clusters of arbitrary sizes and shapes.

The time complexity of DBSCAN is O(n * time to find points within epsilon), where n is the number of data points. In the worst case for high-dimensional data, this complexity is $O(n^2)$. However, in many other cases for low-dimensional data, there are some structures in the data that allow more efficient finding data points within epsilon, which can reduce the time complexity to O(n * log n), which is pretty good.

The memory complexity for DBSCAN is O(n), because the algorithm requires storing only a small amount of data for each data point.

But this algorithm has its drawbacks as well.

Choosing the epsilon can be hard, and this requires good knowledge about the data set we are working with. In order to choose an appropriate epsilon, we can also try different values for the epsilon and compare the results of the clustering thereafter. In many cases, even slight variations of the epsilon value can lead to completely different results.

For example, if the epsilon in our previous task were 1.4, we would get two clusters:

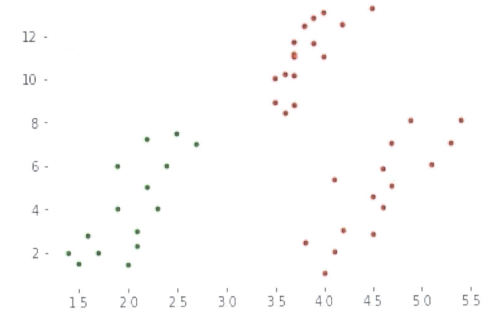

If we increased the epsilon a little bit more to 1.5, there would be only one cluster:

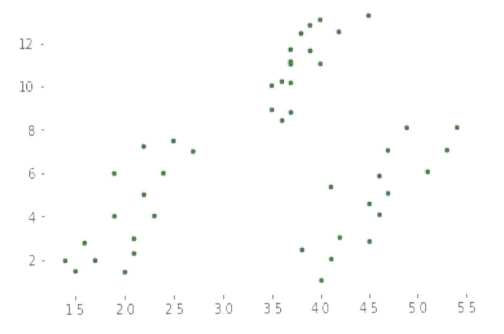

However, if we decreased the epsilon to 1.0, we would again obtain completely different results:

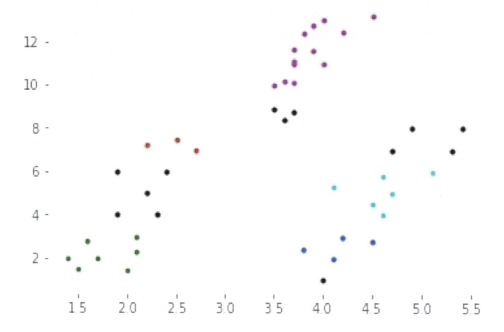

Another disadvantage of DBSCAN is that we can have problems with identifying clusters which have various densities. In such situations, clusters with much lower densities can be discarded as noise.

Neural networks-based clustering

General idea of clustering using artificial neural networks

Recently, artificial neural networks (ANNs) have become an extremely popular computational technique in machine learning. Artificial neural networks are universe function approximaters. Each artificial neural network consists of nodes or neurons which perform a specific function. Therefore, each artificial neural network can be thought of as a function of multiple nested functions.

Different architectures of artificial neural networks can be used for making both labeled and unlabeled modeling.

There have been proposed several types of ANNs with numerous different implementations for clustering tasks. Most of these neural networks apply so-called *competitive learning* rather than error-correction learning as most other types of neural networks do. ANNs used for clustering do not utilize the gradient descent algorithm.

Probably, the most popular type of neural nets used for clustering is called a Kohonen network, named after a prominent Finnish researcher Teuvo Kohonen.

There are many different types of Kohonen networks. These neural networks are very different to most types of neural networks used for supervised tasks. Kohonen networks consist of only two layers.

We will show in detail the principles of functionality of a quite simple Kohonen network. The structure of this neural network is shown below:

output

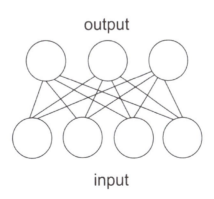

input

As we see, the network consists of two layers: the input layer with four neurons and the output layers with three layers. If you are familiar with neural networks, this structure may look to you like a very simple perceptron. However, this network works in a different way than perceptrons or any other networks for supervised learning, and lucky for us, we don't need any calculus methods when we deal with Kohonen networks.

We will be working with a famous Iris data set, which consists of 150 samples divided into three classes. The data in the dataset must be normalized.

In our neural network, the number of output neurons is equal to the number of clusters or classes (in our case it is three). However, we can construct a more advanced Kohonen network for dealing with problems where we don't know the number of clusters beforehand, but more on that later.

In a Kohonen net, each neuron of an output layer holds a vector whose dimensionality equals the number of neurons in the input layer (in our case it is four). In turn, the number of neurons in the input layer must be equal to the dimensionality of data points given to the network. We will be working with a four-dimensional data set. That is why our network has four neurons in its input layer.

Let's define the vectors of the output layer in our network as w_1, w_2, w_3. These vectors are randomly initialized in a certain range of values.

When the network gets an input, the input is traversed into only one neuron of the output layer, whose value is closer to the input vector than the values of other two output neurons. This neuron is called a winning neuron or the best matching unit (BMU). This is a very important distinction from many other types of neural networks, in which values propagate to all neurons in a succeeding layer. And this process constitutes the principle of competitive learning.

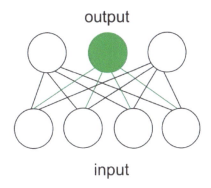

output

input

Let's define the input vectors as x_1, x_2 ... x_n, where n is the number of samples in the training set. In our case, n is 150.

After receiving an input vector x, the winning neuron modifies the value of its previous vector w in a loop according to the formula $w_n = w_n + \lambda (x_n - w_n)$, where λ is a coefficient, which we reduce by $_\Delta\lambda$ in each iteration of the loop unless $\lambda > 0$. We do this for each x in our training set. We can pick input vectors randomly or in a specific order. In this loop, λ and $_\Delta\lambda$ are our parameters, which we define and can modify.

As a result of this algorithm, we have a set of w vectors with new values. So, now our network is trained, and we can start clustering. This is a very simple task: for each vector x we find the closest vector w in our trained neural network. Our x vectors can be even not from our dataset we have worked with. If so, such vectors first have to be normalized.

Constructing a simple neural net for clustering using Numpy arrays

Now, let's code this network in Python.

First, we import all packages we need for this task. This time, we only need Numpy and Pandas:

```python
import numpy as np
import pandas as pd
```

We download the iris data set we will work with and show its first five samples in a data frame:

```python
url = "https://archive.ics.uci.edu/ml/machine-learning-databases/iris/iris.data"
names = ['sepal length', 'sepal width', 'petal length', 'petal width', 'class']
ds = pd.read_csv(url, names=names)
```

```python
ds.head()
```

	sepal length	sepal width	petal length	petal width	class
0	5.1	3.5	1.4	0.2	Iris-setosa
1	4.9	3.0	1.4	0.2	Iris-setosa
2	4.7	3.2	1.3	0.2	Iris-setosa
3	4.6	3.1	1.5	0.2	Iris-setosa
4	5.0	3.6	1.4	0.2	Iris-setosa

We normalize the data and throw them in a numpy array:

```
list_sl=[]
list_sw=[]
list_pl=[]
list_pw=[]
for sl in ds['sepal length']:
    sl = (sl-min(ds['sepal length']))/(max(ds['sepal length'])-min(ds['sepal length']))
    list_sl.append(sl)
for sw in ds['sepal width']:
    sw = (sw-min(ds['sepal width']))/(max(ds['sepal width'])-min(ds['sepal width']))
    list_sw.append(sw)
for pl in ds['petal length']:
    pl = (pl-min(ds['petal length']))/(max(ds['petal length'])-min(ds['petal length']))
    list_pl.append(pl)
for pw in ds['petal width']:
    pw = (pw-min(ds['petal width']))/(max(ds['petal width'])-min(ds['petal width']))
    list_pw.append(pw)

X = np.array( list(zip(list_sl,list_sw, list_pl, list_pw)) )
```

Then, we initiate the number of classes or clusters, the list for the *w* vectors, the number of the *x* vectors, and the dimensionality of the *x* vectors:

```
nc = 3          # number of classes
W = []          # list for w vectors
M = len(X)      # number of x vectors
N = len(X[0])   # dimensionality of x vectors
```

Then, we create a function for obtaining random values for the *x* vectors (or weights), and then we initialize these *x* vectors:

```
def get_weights():
    y = np.random.random() * (2.0 / np.sqrt(M))
    return 0.5 - (1 / np.sqrt(M)) + y
```

```
for i in range(nc):
    W.append(list())
    for j in range(N):
        W[i].append(get_weights() * 0.5)
```

We create a function for computing the Euclidian distance between our *x* and *w* vectors:

```
def distance(w, x):
    r = 0
    for i in range(len(w)):
        r = r + (w[i] - x[i])*(w[i] - x[i])

    r = np.sqrt(r)
    return r
```

We create a function for finding the closest *x* vectors to the *w* vectors:

```
def Findclosest(W, x):
    wm = W[0]
    r = distance(wm, x)

    i = 0
    i_n = i

    for w in W:
        if distance(w, x) < r:
            r = distance(w, x)
            wm = w
            i_n = i
        i = i + 1

    return (wm, i_n)
```

Then, we initialize the λ and $_\Delta\lambda$ coefficients and start looping to find the closest x vectors to the w vectors:

```python
la = 0.3    # λ coefficient
dla = 0.05  # Δλ

while la >= 0:
    for k in range(10):
        for x in X:
            wm = Findclosest(W, x)[0]
            for i in range(len(wm)):
                wm[i] = wm[i] + la * (x[i] - wm[i])

    la = la - dla
```

So, now our network is trained. Finally, we can compare the results of our classification with the actual values from the data frame:

```python
Data = list()

for i in range(len(W)):
    Data.append(list())

dfList = ds['class'].as_matrix()

DS = list()
i = 0
for x in X:
    i_n = Findclosest(W, x)[1]
    Data[i_n].append(x)
    DS.append([i_n, dfList[i]])
    i = i + 1
```

```
print (DS)
```

```
[[0, 'Iris-setosa'], [0, 'Iris-setosa'], [0, 'Iris-setosa'], [0, 'Iris-setosa'], [0, 'Iris-setosa'], [0, 'Iris-setosa'], [0, 'I
ris-setosa'], [0, 'Iris-setosa'], [0, 'Iris-setosa'], [0, 'Iris-setosa'], [0, 'Iris-setosa'], [0, 'Iris-setosa'], [0, 'Iris-set
osa'], [0, 'Iris-setosa'], [0, 'Iris-setosa'], [0, 'Iris-setosa'], [0, 'Iris-setosa'], [0, 'Iris-setosa'], [0, 'Iris-setosa'],
 [0, 'Iris-setosa'], [0, 'Iris-setosa'], [0, 'Iris-setosa'], [0, 'Iris-setosa'], [0, 'Iris-setosa'], [0, 'Iris-setosa'], [0, 'I
ris-setosa'], [0, 'Iris-setosa'], [0, 'Iris-setosa'], [0, 'Iris-setosa'], [0, 'Iris-setosa'], [0, 'Iris-setosa'], [0, 'Iris-set
osa'], [0, 'Iris-setosa'], [0, 'Iris-setosa'], [0, 'Iris-setosa'], [0, 'Iris-setosa'], [0, 'Iris-setosa'], [0, 'Iris-setosa'],
 [0, 'Iris-setosa'], [0, 'Iris-setosa'], [0, 'Iris-setosa'], [0, 'Iris-setosa'], [0, 'Iris-setosa'], [0, 'Iris-setosa'], [0, 'I
ris-setosa'], [0, 'Iris-setosa'], [0, 'Iris-setosa'], [0, 'Iris-setosa'], [0, 'Iris-setosa'], [0, 'Iris-setosa'], [2, 'Iris-ver
sicolor'], [1, 'Iris-versicolor'], [2, 'Iris-versicolor'], [1, 'Iris-versicolor'], [1, 'Iris-versicolor'], [1, 'Iris-versicolo
r'], [1, 'Iris-versicolor'], [1, 'Iris-versicolor'], [1, 'Iris-versicolor'], [1, 'Iris-versicolor'], [1, 'Iris-versicolor'],
 [1, 'Iris-versicolor'], [1, 'Iris-versicolor'], [1, 'Iris-versicolor'], [1, 'Iris-versicolor'], [1, 'Iris-versicolor'], [1, 'I
ris-versicolor'], [1, 'Iris-versicolor'], [1, 'Iris-versicolor'], [1, 'Iris-versicolor'], [1, 'Iris-versicolor'], [1, 'Iris-ver
sicolor'], [1, 'Iris-versicolor'], [1, 'Iris-versicolor'], [1, 'Iris-versicolor'], [1, 'Iris-versicolor'], [1, 'Iris-versicolo
r'], [2, 'Iris-versicolor'], [1, 'Iris-versicolor'], [1, 'Iris-versicolor'], [1, 'Iris-versicolor'], [1, 'Iris-versicolor'],
 [1, 'Iris-versicolor'], [1, 'Iris-versicolor'], [1, 'Iris-versicolor'], [1, 'Iris-versicolor'], [1, 'Iris-versicolor'], [1, 'I
ris-versicolor'], [1, 'Iris-versicolor'], [1, 'Iris-versicolor'], [1, 'Iris-versicolor'], [1, 'Iris-versicolor'], [1, 'Iris-ver
sicolor'], [1, 'Iris-versicolor'], [1, 'Iris-versicolor'], [1, 'Iris-versicolor'], [1, 'Iris-versicolor'], [1, 'Iris-versicolo
r'], [1, 'Iris-versicolor'], [1, 'Iris-versicolor'], [2, 'Iris-virginica'], [1, 'Iris-virginica'], [2, 'Iris-virginica'], [2,
 'Iris-virginica'], [2, 'Iris-virginica'], [2, 'Iris-virginica'], [1, 'Iris-virginica'], [2, 'Iris-virginica'], [2, 'Iris-virgi
nica'], [2, 'Iris-virginica'], [2, 'Iris-virginica'], [1, 'Iris-virginica'], [2, 'Iris-virginica'], [1, 'Iris-virginica'], [2,
 'Iris-virginica'], [2, 'Iris-virginica'], [2, 'Iris-virginica'], [2, 'Iris-virginica'], [2, 'Iris-virginica'], [1, 'Iris-virgi
nica'], [2, 'Iris-virginica'], [1, 'Iris-virginica'], [2, 'Iris-virginica'], [1, 'Iris-virginica'], [2, 'Iris-virginica'], [2,
 'Iris-virginica'], [1, 'Iris-virginica'], [1, 'Iris-virginica'], [2, 'Iris-virginica'], [2, 'Iris-virginica'], [2, 'Iris-virgi
nica'], [2, 'Iris-virginica'], [2, 'Iris-virginica'], [1, 'Iris-virginica'], [1, 'Iris-virginica'], [2, 'Iris-virginica'], [2,
 'Iris-virginica'], [2, 'Iris-virginica'], [1, 'Iris-virginica'], [2, 'Iris-virginica'], [2, 'Iris-virginica'], [2, 'Iris-virgi
nica'], [1, 'Iris-virginica'], [2, 'Iris-virginica'], [2, 'Iris-virginica'], [2, 'Iris-virginica'], [1, 'Iris-virginica'], [2,
 'Iris-virginica'], [2, 'Iris-virginica'], [1, 'Iris-virginica']]
```

We see that the class "2" completely overlaps with the class 'Iris-setosa', the class "1" mostly overlaps with the class 'Iris-versicolor', and the class "0" mostly overlaps with 'Iris-virginica'. There are 18 mismatches between 'Iris-virginica' and 'Iris-versicolor' classes, corresponding to 12% of the entire data set. So, the overall correspondence of our results to the actual data is 88%.

Since we initialized the classes "0", "1", "2" randomly, the order of these classes can be different in other iterations of this program, but it does not change the structure of the classification.

I put up this code on GitHub:

https://github.com/ArtemKovera/clust/blob/master/Kohonen%2Bnetwork%2B.ipynb

Introduction to self-organizing maps

The type of a Kohonen network we have just built works only when we know the number of classes beforehand. In other cases, we should build a more elaborate Kohonen network – such a network is called a self-organizing map (SOM) – that has many output neurons which are topologically connected with each other.

In principle, we can create structures of any dimensions. But the simplest and most practical in most cases structure is a two-dimensional grid of neurons.

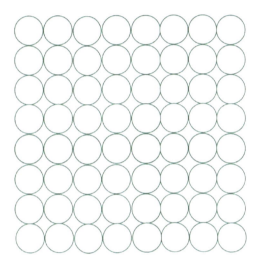

The dimensionality of the structure does not have to be equal to the dimensionality of the feature space. Because of this, self-organizing maps perform not only clustering but at the same time can also perform dimensionality reduction. Also, self-organizing maps are a very powerful tool for data visualization.

The algorithm for training self-organizing maps is quite similar to the one we have just worked with, but it is more complex:

1. Initialize the *w* vectors or weights of our network;
2. Normalize the *x* vectors of the input;
3. Initialize a parameter for time $t = 1$ and set a value for maximum t;
4. Randomly choose any vector *x* from the original data;

5. Find the neuron (vector **w**), which is closest to the vector **x**. This neuron is called the Best Matching Unit (BMU). We denote this neuron by w^{m*}, where $m*$ is the number of this neuron;

6. Change all the coefficients of neurons' vectors **w** according to the following formula: $w^m = w^{mn} + \eta(t)h(t, \rho(m, m*))[x-w^m]$, where $\eta(t) = \eta 0exp(-at)$, $h(t, \rho) = exp[-(\rho 2)/(2\sigma(t))]$, $\sigma(t) = \sigma 0exp(-bt)$. Here, $\rho(m, m*)$ denotes the distance in the neuron arrangement geometry on the plane for the neuron numbered m and $m*$;

7. $t = t + 1$;

8. If the maximum t is exceeded, then stop the algorithm;

9. Go to the step 4.

Also, there can be many other possible variations of the algorithm for SOMs with some additional steps and slight changes.

In this algorithm, the values for **a**, **b**, and the maximum value for **t** are our parameters, which we can modify.

After building and training a SOM, we can use it. For any vector **x**, we determine the nearest neuron, and its location will show the region on the map to which this vector belongs.

We can put on the map many data points and after that can use the k-means or any other algorithm to cluster these data point.

Thank you for getting this book!

I hope, now you understand the clustering algorithms better.

If you are interested in artificial intelligence..

As you probably know, machine learning is an integral part of artificial intelligence. Modern AI systems are primarily based on machine learning. If you are interested in artificial intelligence, you can read my previous, introductory book *"How to Create Machine Superintelligence"*. It is a totally conceptual book, which doesn't contain any code nor math formulas. In that book, we will go over the following topics:

➢ Basics of computational complexity;

➢ Some ideas on the capabilities of natural and artificial intelligence;

➢ Basics of classical computing and different types of computer architecture;

➢ Basic principles of quantum computing;

➢ Basics of artificial neural networks;

➢ Some general ideas on building general AI and dealing with a control problem.